ABSENCE WHERE AS
(CLAUDE CAHUN AND THE UNOPENED BOOK)

Nathanaël (Nathalie Stephens)

NIGHTBOAT BOOKS : NEW YORK : 2009

L'eau court dans les ruisseaux. Lâchez sur *moi* vos chiens. JE coule dans les rues, me love en leurs fontaines . . . Ici les eaux dormantes . . . la grande inondation. Ici sont exposés les vivants . . . Et les morts, les intrus, dans mon miroir de poche, vont-ils vous reconnaître?

— Claude Cahun, *Confidences au miroir*

The water runs in the streams. Unleash your dogs on ME. I run through the streets, coil in their fountains . . . Here the sleeping waters . . . the great flood. Here the living are exposed . . . And the dead, the intruders, in my pocket mirror, will they recognise you?

— Claude Cahun, *Confidences au miroir*, trans. N.S.

FA ILLE

(1) Envoi

I will speak to you of a *relation*, possibly of a *liaison*, most certainly of a *correspondence*. Here, at the outset, what measure of concupiscence, of ardor, of intemperance, comes to regulate, if not deregulate, my thought – the movement that will propel it, in time and in spite of time; the narrative that isn't one, for having been anticipated; the affective reserve of this undertaking, this questioning, this insatiate desire that announces every encounter, every exchange, every reach, whose wager is released with impunity, and immediately recuperated by a body ligatured to a historical, sensual, clearly cleaved, (momentous) moment, eliminating it from the place toward which it rushes, the mouth by which it imagines itself to be practised, the tongue that invites its frustration, the story that dares to narrate it.

Of the relational, most of all I retain defeat. Of liaison, departure. Of correspondence, flight. Of offering, the hand, empty, emptied.

At the outset, I hesitate. The uncalculated, uncalculatable part, agitated, detached from the place from which it is propelled and toward which it goes, is uncomfortably settled in the liminal space of the *envoi*, the gesture soliciting an other, the proximity inadvertently availed of such an inclination.

Trampled, scarred, derailed.

Before even risking ourselves, we are called upon to gauge these capricious disturbances, to say yes, and what's more, however. To undertake the determining disposition of place, its arrangement, and the body, abandoned there, constituted as it is of nothing but the senses (and sensuality), feels, in this, the incensed, senseless, assails itself. Desirous, it attempts to express its dislocation, intent on joining what escapes it quite simply, but not without first seizing (upon) it. And how? By a *resonance*. Which augments and amplifies it, sounds it, prolongs and empties it out, mistakes it. Impossible now to go back, or else yes : with the knowledge that what badgers from behind awaits somewhere else without consideration. The circle does not close, which does not preclude our being inescapably enclosed within it.

I insist on that which is liminal, delineates and distends, distorts and denies. What imposes itself littorally if not laterally between two places (at least). What escapes us, and from which we do not escape.

Correspondence for flight. Liaison for bait. Relation for strain. Doubtful. Undoubtedly.

I make (myself) : envoi.

(2) Letters

It is possible to write one's day through letters, a letter. It should
come as no surprise then, that I have formerly attached myself
in friendship, in literature, in sensuality, to a personage out of
context, out of place (out of my mind), away from *here*, this
present, both inhabited and uninhabitable, imposed and
suffered, decided and nil; preferring an obsessive, perverse,
voluptuous *dislocation*, to superficial, exposed, pedantic
actuality : what is so crassly referred to as the *everyday*. To
render myself elsewhere in order to extract myself from
the place, from the moment riveted to its materiality, the
architectured, temporal space made precise by a name, an
arrangement of buildings cobbled onto a dismantled hori-
zon, a situation, a location, a *there*.

There where I put my hand. *There* where I close the
door behind me. *There* where I unpack my bag. *There* where
place incites me, chides me, invites me.

I breathe, smother, burst, away.

A constituent *there* whose edification rests on a spatial
foundation implicating the body and topography, letters and
history, sexuation and politics. An unfounded foundation,
bluntly administered, in other words imbued with latent
aggressivity, an aggressivity that suffuses the skeleton of the
cities through which we move, the languages that silence
us. Torn, ruptured, gaping. The breach made so violently

5

opens that which, plunged into muteness, would not otherwise have known (how) to express itself. Institutes the unstamped letter, the suspended call, accuses the emptiness.

In 1997, I addressed these words to Colette : *Ce plaisir de te déguster au-delà du temps et de la littérature, où ma démarche solitaire à la tienne se joint comme un filament argenté au coeur de l'offre rivé.* And : *Colette délie-moi, ouvre-toi que je respire encore d'un souffle non-contaminé, d'une vie intacte et déréglée. Donne-moi ta peau que je te lise telle que tu es, sans miroir, sans distorsion, sans reflet, au fond d'un paysage discret.*[1] Uninhabitable present, unspeakable (unforgiveable?) language; I retreated into the (Utopian) oneiric space of a (poetic) *jardin des rêves*, whose permeable limits did not preclude violation in the least, and whose very constitution rested on a concept of slippage away from a desperately solicited place.

---

[1]*Colette m'entends-tu?* Laval, TROIS, 1997. (*The pleasure of savouring you outside of time and of literature, where my solitary gait is joined to yours like a silver filament at the heart of the offer contained. [...] Colette untie me, open me that I may breathe once more with uncontaminated breath, an intact and disordered life. Give me your skin that I may read you as you are, without mirrors, without distortion, without reflection, deep in a discrete landscape.*) Translations are mine, unless indicated otherwise.

On the subject of Gide, I affirmed just as insistently : *J'apprends à lire les mains vides, à laisser la place à l'ennui. Je ne veux pas ce que veut Gide, ce qu'il a voulu. Même si de lui j'ai appris à vouloir.* And what's more : *Gide n'était pas dupe. Il savait que le possible demeurait possible du moment où il ne tentait rien.*[2] In order to locate myself : otherwise. To make of dislocation the very place, not only of annihilation, but of survival, yoked to what, of itself, is most fragile : the uncontestable breakage that comprises it, the rupture with normative temporality. A suffocation that determines breathing. The aberration of an uncontested a priori of existence.

---

[2]*Je Nathanaël*, Montréal, L'Hexagone, 2003. (*I am learning to read empty handed, to leave room for boredom. I do not want what Gide wants, wanted. Even if from him I learned to want. […] Gide was not a dupe. He knew that a thing remained possible so long as it remained unattempted.*) (English self-translation published by BookThug as *Je Nathanaël*, 2006.)

(3) The other JE

Je est un autre wrote yet an other. This is no protest. But it does happen that alongside this assertion, I ask myself what it is about this *other* no longer set in opposition to the *je*, but who becomes the *je*. Who does not offer, but assumes a presence, who is imposed, superimposed onto the *self*, onto that very frivolous, very uncalculated *je*, so untiringly *je*, thus corrupting *l'amour-propre* proper, by making of the self, which is to say the *other*, the antecedent that obliterates with impunity.

A JE that doesn't shirk responsibility by attributing to an *other* the weight of that voice, the breath of that commitment, the force of that reach; but a confused, unsettled, unhabituated JE, in a perpetual state of slippage, materialised and extinguished by the same movement that extends and reduces, indistinct from the other who approaches without intimation, who makes of presence, misunderstanding, and renders inevitable the defeat of the thing against which no self can be erected, and toward which none can go by rights. Where the usual bearings have disbanded, where the question is no longer one of legitimacy or protest, where place is granted reprieve and indivisible while cleaved.

(4) The book that comes to me

I will speak to you of the constitution of a library. The arrangement of several dozen books on a shelf far from here, that is far from the place where we find ourselves at present, which not so long ago constituted my own present, but which is already distant, in another place, traversed by several places at once, which, together, are muddied by a scrawl of trajectories accomplished altogether frenetically. I say this in order that you might situate what cannot, in effect, be situated; in order that you might name, furtively and incompletely, this thing which refuses itself a name.

In 2003, I unpacked my bags in Montréal at the moment at which the need to leave again presented itself irremediably. From place to place I attempted to refute the impermeable notion of place, from the mountains of western Canada, through several large U.S. cities, the north-east then the south-west of England, all the way to the Basque and Catalan countries. In the span of a year, I walked on ground bordering the Atlantic, the North Sea, the Mediterranean and the Bay of Biscay, and this chronology of travels dipped into all of those waters transformed itself into a moving mass that I dragged all the way to Chicago, where, beneath the thieving sky at the centre of a continent plied by filthy greed, I re-placed books erupting from boxes burst apart from so many moves.

Last summer, I set my study up in a room I have since aban-doned. With each move, the books find new placements. With several exceptions, one of which is the subject of this essay.

The constitution of the shelf visible from my work table is determining. There are those books whose selection is governed by an affective consideration – my attachment to an author, a period of time, a place, encounter, a sensibility – without neglecting the importance of a text in my trajec-tory, the impulses that formulate it. Mourning, melancholy, languor, desires, perversions and languages find themselves juxtaposed without any reason other than that which I grant them, capriciously, intentionally. Benjamin can very easily frequent *Le Basque de Poche*; Ann Quin, Ugrešić; Nelson Algren, Catherine Mavrikakis; Lispector, Koltès; Beckett, Sarah Kofman; Darwish, Pizarnik. One never knows, and what is an indispensable accompaniment can from one day to the next become intolerable, whence the necessity for turn-over, renewal. To each place its markers, its demands, which only reveal themselves at the moment of the installation, of both body and furniture, and not a minute before. Books, like artworks, are the last elements to find their place – in transit, in passing, from their dispersal to their *de*rangement.

In East Anglia, my shelves remained empty. Impossible to place a single tome without evoking the terror of the tomb. There, emptiness was more fitting.

To each rule its exception. Comprising the constitutive elements of a parenthesis, placed at the two ends of this very aleatory assemblage of texts drawn from the pile muddling the floor, two books found a provisionally permanent place there, in other words for the duration of the occupation of my study on Division Street : precisely five months. At the rightmost end, purporting to close the system which isn't much of one : a grid-papered notebook, recently acquired from the Art Institute of Chicago, with an electric blue cover reproducing a detail of Renzo Piano's plans for the Modern Wing of the museum. A notebook, still in its wrapper, where no mark or trace are inscribed.

At the leftmost end, the textual gesture that inaugurates the movement of the whole collection, the book I am coming to, and which comes to me to introduce disturbances and recriminations into my work space, fateful reminder of disjunction and disappearance – of erasure – that mastodon, *Écrits*, by writer and photographer Claude Cahun, which, since it has been following me, pursuing me, remains *unopened*. At any rate until the moment at which I agreed to speak of it, to open what had remained closed, in other words what was inevitable and unbearable, but so imperative.[3]

---

[3]*Absence Where As* first took the form of a talk delivered in February 2006 in Martine Delvaux's graduate seminar at l'Université du Québec à Montréal on *La photo/biographie et la sexuation*. Entitled *L'Absence au lieu*, it was

Two unopened books, full of promise, the last of which contains not a trace, and the first of which, imperious, remains to be read. Two milestones, so to speak, opening onto the unlimited, unapproached space of what I will allow myself to call literature. All of which – and not least myself – governed from the spine of a book that is not Cahun's because it is not "signed" Claude Cahun, whose impressive trajectory is already amply known, said to be *one-of-a-kind*, and whose impudent, disapproving, certainly intransigent stare is start-lingly, singularly, dreadfully, desperately *familiar*.

.

subsequently published as a book-length essay, commissioned by Patrick Poirier for Nota Bene, under the Nouveaux Essais Spirale imprint (Québec, 2007). I owe each a debt of gratitude for having nudged the work into its various forms, and to Catherine Mavrikakis to begin with.

Anne Malena, Jeff Marlin, M., Stephen Motika, and Sina Queyras were incomparable correspondents during various stages of the work on the English language text.

(5) Decay for decry

I admit to closing more books than I open. What does this
say if not that literature, the writing I make of my life, the
space to which I have unbearably consigned myself, *bids*
me, forbids me? That the book, the one I would reach for
as much as the one I would write, puts me off, resists me,
diminishes, misuses, decries me. When, confronted with
the textual, the corporeal recognises, ceases to recognise
itself, and reading, rereading, derailing, become indistin-
guishable from one another and invite immoderation, call
up the body cobbled onto the palpable abstract until it is
made insufferable; and the exposed text wreaks of vomit
for having been too many times swallowed back, spat up,
absorbed, engulfed, rendered. Unbearable relationship –
for having been maintained and slavered over – of body
to text, of book to bone, spit to trace, hand to indecision.
Abjection before the in-spite-of-everything, the all-against
which reveals itself within, or is at very least imbued, and
as a result inextricable, smothered, and whose simultaneity
inhabits, paralyses, obstructs and censures just as it is be-
ing inhabited, paralysed, obstructed and censured. Resists
the occupation that grants the impression of unoccupying
what wants so much – what *demands* – to manifest itself
furiously, wants to disavow, to display, to dessicate ... what?
Its *place* : its morbid, insinuated place, hooking into tendons
tying the bone to its verb, the marrow to its verve, raging

(6) Senses and sentences

The evocation of Colette, Gide, and now Cahun, suggests the establishment of a lineage I would like at once to abolish, or at very least refute. Not so long ago, I pointed to the minute distance between la famille (family) and la fa ille (fault line ... flaw ... rift).[5] I return to it today because it is of primary importance to reject straightaway this possibility, so well anchored in our psycho-social reflexes, of the *intrinsic* bond to the other by some ideology of parentage, where biological authority predominates (the etymology of the word family refers curiously and not surprisingly to servitude). I am not speaking of blood, I wish to make that clear. Not of blood, but of the *senses*, if not *sensuality*. Although the tendency does inhabit us, I myself am not immune, and remain as vigilant as possible.

By lineage, I mean both the trace, that is the line strictly speaking, the one that yokes the body to temporality, that fixes its trajectory, refusing in this way the aleatory, the un-expected, the furtive and misunderstood place of *encounter*;

---

[5]*Fold* (inédit). See *Tessera*, Vol. 33-34 (Winter 2003). For example: "You point to the short distance between la famille and la fa ille. You live in the place between two letters. You are in your quarry at nightfall and you are picking through stones in darkness falling into that familiar emptiness, that impossible place where your name slips from your tongue to shatter against rock. It wasn't yours to begin with."

and filiation, bloody lineage, which would have individuals bound, through membership, transmitted by a decisive social mythology, to some clan : what we tend to refer to as *family*, thus inscribing a rigid attitude toward the other, for it presupposes an *origin*, an *order* of things, a fixed and prior place toward which to return, or turn about, that is turn one's back to the other toward whom we are incumbent to go in order to break the lie of predetermined membership.

Relational rigidity underpinned by a monotheistic posture governing the very minute details of our (Western), supposedly secular societies, rejecting the manifold in favour of the singular – of the locatable. Cult of the origin, the originary, of clan and outcome – of a beginning and an end. Cult of the rock before water, which, despite armatures and dams, reinforcements, will erode even the hardest of surfaces. Suppression of the desire that spills from the body in which it is meant to remain enclosed, unseated, silenced. Refusal of plurality, of permeability, of vagueness. Cult of exactitude. Refusal, finally, of disintegration, of the unknown ... who comes to me.

What can I offer in response other than this : that I maintain here, *in this place* where I am, in this book that drains (from) me, the right to *disorder*. I do not wish to perpetuate the absolutism of blood, nor the organisation, the systematisation of human relations, of senses and impulses, but to suggest that the disorder emerging from an irreparable breach opened in the elusive, furtive matter that is the self, the JE evoked earlier, leads to *fortuitous* encounters that are both past and insistent, operating all at once the materialisation, the destabilisation and the disintegration of the place that might be thought to be definitive, the lines – architectural, corporeal, geographical, linguistic, sexual – that impose themselves definitively; of matter, in sum, that is immaterial, furtive and imbued.

For, and I will return to this, the fatalism governing the artificial boundaries erected between beings and things, beings and words, bordering the senses and delineating territories, themselves affected, is gorged with aggressivity and has but one word on its tongue : no.

(7) Return

"Où sont mes sensations?" asks Cioran. "Elles se sont éva-nouies en . . . moi, et ce moi qu'est-il, sinon la somme de ces sensations évaporées."[6] These words recall the echo emerging from a void whose vacancy, whose absence of content, attest to a linguistic void that can only express want, absence, retreat; that is capable of saying *nothing*. A voiceless echo whose generative call is nowhere locatable, other than in the self, having already escaped in the same turn that would have positioned it *there*. An echo, then, that resembles neither itself – because once projected it is transformed, deformed – nor the imitated sound, for being swallowed again immediately, ushered away from . . . me. An echo, that is, a reply, that doesn't tender a response, and whose trace disappears at the very moment of its generation.

Voiceless echo, bodiless voice, unarticulated mouth. Hollowing the encounter is a drain, and the absence, assimilated to the echo to which the echo returns, absence, in other words lacuna and want, *overflows* with insufficiency, mine foremost, and place itself, which seems incapable of sustaining me, of holding me here, of offering, from the

---

[6] E. M. Cioran, *De l'inconvénient d'être né*, Paris, Gallimard, 1973. (*Where are my sensations? They have vanished in . . . my self, and what is this self, if not the sum of these evaporated sensations?*)

fragile breath of desire, an inhabited *somewhere*, replete, and in which to be situated.

Obsessive dislocation of the body before the book that supplants place, that becomes the only possible place, that embodies and disperses it. The anguish so often evoked before the blank page is but the transposition of the body in movement immobilised by a thing whose inertia is betrayed by all the possible displacements it assumes and inculcates to this body burning with impatience to move over new terrain. Movement that must be undertaken without batting an eye, without moving from one end to the other of even the smallest of rooms, where the table is its only available support for the convergence of all the other possible places, all of which are : denied. It is not, then, the unwritten page that provokes this sort of madness of interrupted movement, but the body severed from its trajectory, severed from the place into which it would want to pour itself. From the place (the text, not the page, which is little more than an exhausted symbol, excessively mourned by Romantic affect, that subsists today in the fixed expressions stupidly governing literature); severed, then, from the place into which it would want to pour itself, from the place stirred by the language that would silence it and whose removal is the very same echo that alludes to me.

This absence fulfills expectation, incites me to the aporia with which I come to identify. The sound that comes to me is the one I was wanting (for). The trajectory the one I had imagined. The unfurled wave salvages and drowns. It is enough to see sideways for all the (im)possible outcomes to deploy themselves, for me to go after them and for them to mislead me. *There* where I wish to go. *There* where I (JE) do not.

scribed by the question: *Where am I?* Even more pressingly than *why*. I imagine myself in some building, a substitute for language, from which I am violently expulsed, and the walls against which I lean are ploughed by a storm, a shell, a cyclone, a tremor, whose (linguistic) shrapnel riddles me with prefabricated formulations, inculcates a denatured, fraudulent, morbid gait. Liberated from the building that had come only to signify circumscription, I raise my eyes onto a sky whose name escapes me but which reveals itself already to have been named, in other words conquered, underpinned and *specified*. Before the immensity of the thing, I disappear, but insufficiently, such that I am recuperated by the one who anticipates me competitively, grinds me, hammers me, seduces and rivals me, *underhands* me.

Fractured fa ille, the swollen tongue hooking on the remains of which it might otherwise settle, in breach of conduct, excised, split. *There*, exactly where I glimpsed her, that unlike-myself, where I have yet to draw up a letter from this leftover m, disappeared and immoderate, who, by her absence, holds me, withholds me and that I hold in my hands, mute manifestation of misunderstanding mine(d) and missing. A letter I have yet to read-write and whose tide, plunged deep inside, submerges, unfurls and drowns me. An apprehended letter that writes itself from me, is written despite me and that I don't write, from the moment at which *there* I rest my eyes, see, see (for) myself.

L'auteures

(9) Dead time

All this time we are seated – (s)he is in fact standing – Claude Cahun and I, so to speak, across from one another.[7] The resemblance is troubling. And this, for several reasons. First, this resemblance, whether imagined or real, presupposes a memory that does not exist, cannot exist. *I don't remember her. I have no reason to remember her. Because it happens that we are very distinctly indistinct (s)he and I.* This resemblance is not only physiological; it goes far beyond the lines of the face, the quality of the stare, the sensibility projected from the photograph. There are the biographical details, Cahun's ideological engagement, artistic contribution, indefinite gender, her judeity, even the fragility of her health. There is also the fact of the French language, and England. Some might take comfort in such proximity, a narrative from which to enlarge one's own. This is not at all my experience. On the contrary. I feel dread verging on madness.

How can I put it? In her, I *resemble* myself. Not : I recognise myself. But *resemble* myself. There is no longer

---

[7]*She*, when referring to Cahun, or to myself, might just as easily be *he*, splitting (apart) the binary with annulling reversal. For when the two *correspond*, here, disappear, when their *I*'s touch, I like to think that one and the same turn into some other, nameless, name. I keep to *her* for the sake of unconstancy. Julian T. Brolaski is a *correspondent inégalable* in these and other matters pertaining to the selfe.

distinction, but indistinction. There is no longer differen-tiation, nor even difference, but absorption. Even more – or less – than this, there is subtraction, and not accretion as one might think, subtraction of one from the other, subtrac-tion that results in the erasure, the nullification of the two of us.

The photograph offers itself as an abyss.[8]

Photography represents dead time. In this instance, it also offers false passage. Because the visceral recognition, catapulted into *resemblance*, is inevitably disappointing, and for this reason : it invites the void, it seduces nothingness. It opens a door only to close it at once, abandoning me agape before the thing offered freely and with the illusion of its totality, torn immediately away such that I find myself ask-ing whether this encounter did indeed take place, if the pos-sibility of this encounter might realistically be envisioned, if not formulated, away from the sole desire that may have

---

[8]The photograph wrapped around Claude Cahun's *Écrits* shows her alone. The photograph has been cropped. In the uncropped image, Cahun is ac-companied – and in a public space. (S)he is standing in front of a bookshop, in the street, on the occasion of the launch of *Aveux non avenus*. There are not just (s)he and the lens in a closed and performative space characteristic of the many "self-portraits"; there is a woman whose identity is unknown (perhaps the bookshop owner), who has been excised from the photograph and to whom no reference is made ; there is also the *other* (an *autre moi*) who stares at her *exposed*, and who *takes* her photograph. The *other* for whom we, voyeures, become substitutes, whose place I take, replace myself).

provoked it. And the urgent question : whence this desire, and why?

The problem of photography, of this photograph, is aporetic. It invites and repels. It evokes and crosses out. There is not only encounter, but *collapse*. There is *casting* and recasting. Of one (*me*) onto the other (*(s)he*), immediately laid over the self, echoed, propagated, and swallowed back, bringing about a fall toward disappearance. The photograph is *echo*. It sends me back to what, of myself, I am already projecting, in the perpetual doubling of stares and faces; there is nullification, there is the total and totalitarian achievement of the absence to which I am confronted, to which I *owe it to myself* to be confronted. Absence of being and place, of voice and trace. There is the erasure of memory – hers and mine – that provokes the erasure of the (personal) past, and even of history. There is not only erasure but refutation. There is annihilation. By our two presences, *ad vitam aeternam*, what amounts to *never again*, we make the *avowal* of our *resemblance*. One and other we cease. Through this exchange, this relationship, this liaison, this *correspondence*, we confirm the implacability of lineage, because it is, at the moment of exchanged glances, inevitable – as well as its incapacity. The generative movement, so to speak, begun by the resemblance, the *I resemble myself*, directly incites its abatement. When, before her, *before her photograph*, I say JE, I cease.

(1 0) Transport

"Se reproduire est disparaître" writes Georges Bataille.[9] A paradox of positions. *To reproduce oneself is to disappear.*

Photography is spectral, we know this already, but the spectre remains nonetheless a presence with which to contend, before which to position oneself, to rush at if necessary, or else flee. The spectre calls to mind the existence of what no longer is, in the materiality of the projected image. In the relationship I am describing, to this photograph in particular, *we haven't even the right to death.* The doubling evoked earlier borders on submersion, closing itself at once over the thing toward which it is propelled. Bataille's words could be modified thus : *To resemble oneself is to disappear.* Absolute disappearance and without end. Taken up with each look that falls upon the book, reiterated in perpetual refusal and impossibility.

But what is this refusal? What is this impossibility? Where does this desire come from? And why irreparable? What of the . . . unopened . . . book? Its prohibition. The singular absence that is the text that denies us, and that we deny, at the outset. *That I deny myself.* The problematic is at very least of a linguistic nature, that is, it is not yoked to the

---

[9]*La littérature et le mal*, Paris, Gallimard, 1957.

fact of the book, to the object in itself, but to the *idea* of the book, to the text that steals away from it, from us, from the very language that would hold it *here*, legible.

In *Le livre du vivant*, Jabès has Sarah say : "Et je n'ai qu'un souhait à formuler. Puisses-tu ne jamais voir ce que je vois."[10] A mad dwelling, this language by which she would express herself, the interred oblivion to which she is consigned, sublimated in a cry from which she will not emerge, because "Je n'entends pas le cri, dit Sarah. Je suis le cri."[11] Unfathomable madness that nonetheless saturates the unpronounceable utterance, the uninhabitable dwelling, the thing of horror toward which she goes, mouth wide, obliterated, in which she dies, incapable of death. From her judeity, revivified by the unaccomplished, fugitive cry, the body into which speech is absorbed, swallowed back, un-expressed; a suffocation which leads her to say to, to want, for the lover who is refused her by the Shoah and the charge of her femininity: "Puisses-tu ne jamais voir ce que je vois."

---

[10]Edmond Jabès, *Le livre de Questions*, Paris, Gallimard, 1963-65. ("And I have only one wish: that you may never see what I see." Trans. Rosmarie Waldrop, *The Book of Questions*, Middletown (CT), Wesleyan University Press, 1976.)

[11]*Ibid*. ("I do not hear the scream, said Sarah. I am the scream." Trans. Rosmarie Waldrop.)

Not the invisible, but the unimaginable, the too-visible, un-expected, aghast. A voice indissociable from its corporeality, inexpressible for having pronounced it, the walling in of the manacled truth against which she can do nothing, but that she would spare the lover who intimates it for having borne it at her sides, absent, remembered. In *Le livre du vivant*, the inexhaustible exhaustion comes to an end, unending. Hope has us speak it in echo, the insane hope of escape, but it is too late : we are the living breach, the breach is me. "Puisses-tu ne jamais voir ce que je vois."

It is impossible for me – for those of us who are look-ing – to approach this photograph without being accosted by the History of the 20th century. Because Claude Cahun's stare comes to us from the past whose end, whose horror, whose inflexibility, whose insolubility, we now appreciate[12]– just as we ignore it, deny it *determinedly*; (s)he looks at us, not only from the spine of a book, but from the abyss of history. Her eyes accuse her era and our . . . posthumous . . . complicity. "La vérité" warns Simone Weil "est du côté de la mort."[13] But what is this death? And what truth?

---

[12]With all of the (disturbed and disturbing) attendant economic connota-tions of *appreciation*.

[13]Simone Weil, *La pesanteur et la grâce*, Paris, Plon, 1947/1988. (Truth is on the side of death. Trans. Emma Crawford, *Gravity and Grace*, Routledge, 2002.)

"There is no document of culture which is not at the same time a document of barbarism."[14] This admonishment obliges to a certain muteness, to a stammer unremittingly harped on by the present. Not only does it remove membership to a language, a country – whose borders we know to be arbitrary and artificial – but to the *place* where we find ourselves. We are transported, far from here, *elsewhere*, and once we've arrived, once we've put our bags down, arranged the furniture, shelved the books, learned the language, place slides out from under once again. The movement – the reach – toward the *other* – the other place, the other being, the other language, the other context – rescinds itself while finding formulation. From the degree zero to ground zero is the place, so to speak, the moment where we are : razed. The erasure of that which is underway. The photograph of Cahun calls this sharply to attention : *Tu as beau te récrier: le lieu où tu te dis naître n'existe pas.*[15] Not : *no longer* exists, as I had once accused, but *doesn't* exist. Never existed.

Closed, the book cannot betray. The promise cannot be granted. Opening remains possible. The trajectory, yet

---

[14]Walter Benjamin, *Selected Writings, Volume 4, 1938-1940*, eds. Howard Eiland and Michael W. Jennings, trans. Harry Zohn, Cambridge (MA), Harvard University Press, 2003/2006.

[15]*Underground*, Laval, TROIS, 1999. (*Cry as you will : the place you claim to come from does not exist.*) Reiterated with slight distortion.

unbegun, remains to be undertaken. It is still possible to believe in the lure of arrival. In the redemption of History. In the plenitude that would result from it. In our full participation. In the place, henceforth unoccupied, that awaits. In the voluptuousness of speech. The fervour of the caress. In the expanse of language, of the expression attached to it. In other words, in the freedom that has been promised for always, and denied, but for which we are responsible, despite ourselves, and always, to seize upon—

(11) Failure

—but we know all too well that, not only is the place un-
available, it doesn't even exist, it hasn't grounds to exist : it
is offered by the same gesture that withdraws it. Closed, the
book *can only betray*. The porosity of the book divulges the
expanse of nothingness that awaits it – that awaits us. Open
or closed, it accuses us read or unread, the wager is the same.
The place you claim to come from – the place toward which you
reach – this place – does not exist. Not because its material-
ity is denied, but because *the very idea of its materiality* is
formulated by a language – this one or another – which
does to us what the photograph of Cahun does to me. It
projects us into devastating unrest, offering no escape, the
way out is both free and obstructed, in other words : disap-
peared. As in the Sartrian hell, the door is wide open, but
there is no veritable exit; there is nowhere to go; the bridges
are burned, the sidewalks catastrophied. The stare carried
across from the other century calls us to ourselves, makes us
say JE again with the awareness that the irrecuperable past
is gaining, has caught up with us; that our *presence* in the
present is elusive; that the place we flee runs from us as well;
that the desired escape route leads to an even deeper abyss
where, at the moment at which we exercise *resemblance*, bind
ourselves, so to speak, in the photographic image we make
of ourselves, we participate fully, with or without consent, in
the violent opening of a breach in the unfathomable matter

of being and place, neither of which can exist; neither for us nor for anyone else. Again and again we cross the threshold of the void. Again and again, our eyes meet. Again and again we reach with certainty toward that thing which, untiringly, irremediably, does not exist, not because it has ceased to exist, but because it cannot exist, having never, in its becoming, *been*, because the movement by which it might have been released is the same movement that will ensure its annihilation. By saying JE, by claiming membership, to a particular place, to a historical moment, to some *relation*, we fulfill its finality, we formulate the words that will silence the word we await despite ourselves, with stupor, in the emptiness of waiting, which is none other than the dizzying history of disappearance.

THE THERE

(1 2) Grind to see

Here I am this visage, this face that comes to me at my work table deploying everything against which I thought I had guarded. What is there to do other than pick up the pieces, the remains, the scraps, the fragments and shards, the disintegrated particles, the decomposition of the thing against which I was leaning, the place where I was? Gather for discard, hold for tarnish, read for rot. Drawn into the butchery that awaits, summons and stalks me, the exposed part, its hazardous combination of places and languages that return me by chance and with impunity to myself, to the place that pulverises me, to the look I desire, to the disappearance, the death, the end, of the interminable refrain of the *there*, fissured enclosure where I drain, accumulate, crumble, disperse, where I am incessantly repatriated, stateless, unsettled, deserter, deserted.

(13) Too great a distance

The epistolary gesture was to have spared me the struggle with Klee's *Angelus Novus* (or so I thought), that angel of history whose care is entrusted through Benjamin's "On the Concept of History" and to which we are to some degree consigned, angel of history if not of death, or at very least angel incapacitated before the death that puts on the face of the future toward which he is irrevocably and blindly precipitated. The letter would crush the uninhabitable present, the unlocatable place, in favour of a past – manifold and paradoxically unbegun – that would overtake itself by arriving as far as *here*, where I summon it : *there* where I would join (to) it, in the unreadable and unconditioned space between two bodies – books, lovers, geographies – rooted to the very movement that throws them out, overthrows them. *The letter would indicate : too great a distance.*

And yet madness intrudes at the very moment at which the body can no longer tell itself from another, can no longer tell its constitutive dislocation, can't tell the differences required of it. Where the *letters*, all genres taken together, dog-eared and stained, worn and transcribed, are laid over the bodies that receive them and to which they are tendered, sent, dissolve.

For antecedence (whether, besides filiation, the photographic impression or the text of a handwritten letter) renders us residual. Fixes itself in time in this way, even as a fugitive pushing the ground away from her feet, exchanging herself indifferently against places and languages, against various manifestations of the same that hold her back, because always in relation to whatever it is (s)he has just quit – without ever calling it quits. (S)he is never done discarding, and inevitably entangled. I am the scrap of what precedes me. I am the aftermath of the history that invented, conceived me, modeled, configured, inverted me, anything but : free. In the words of Kristeva: *Tous déchets, tous cadavres.*[16]

It is not a matter, here, of retreat into a deterministic, fatalistic posture – a disengaged and anesthetised position – but the affirmation, the observation, that presence is a *consequence*, inhabited by layers of absence of which we are one and none.

I am before Cahun's photograph as before Cocteau's mirror; but *here*, the effect is akin to import, perhaps even *deport*, but it is not one of transport, elation. I am snatched up by it, by this photograph that ruthlessly divines me, mines me. A plane and abyssal surface, the photograph does not reflect, it swallows. It cannibalises its subject as well as

---

[16]Julia Kristeva, *Soleil noir. Dépression et mélancolie*, Paris, Gallimard, 1987. (Waste and cadavers all. Trans. Leon S. Roudiez, *Black Sun: Depression and Melancholia*, New York, Columbia University Press, 1989.)

(s)he – in this instance me – who looks, who dares to look, who risks herself by looking, by adopting the proposed trajectory, which is one of exhaustion, of interminable exhaustion, approaching a relentless *inferno* of looking.

Is it even necessary to reiterate the resulting paralysis, the fascination, the terror, the excitement, emotion? The invitation, which is not without wager, has a Faustian stench about it. I end up floundering in what is not mine to suffuse but nonetheless seizes me, removes and relates me in a language sufficiently approximate that I lend myself to it without realising it (or myself). Without noticing what disappears, without realising that it is incomprehensible and holds no place for me, that it offers itself in exchange, but that this offer is fallacious because the substitution operates an erasure in favour of what it would otherwise preserve : the thing that disappears. The photograph accomplishes an abduction – a seizure.

It assimilates one and other, one to the other : Cahun, me. Here, there.

(1 4) The residual and nothingness

A small detour now, to return to the scene of flight, (re)situate myself in relation to that limit or border governing all crossings, by instigating a material blockage, and while determined, altogether aleatory, which reproduces and manifests itself, catches (us) at the turning point in ourselves, in the space that is our own, the place from which we might risk saying JE, if it weren't denied us, prohibited. A gestural and expressive JE, linguistic and corporeal. Interiority entangled with a geography of hindrance. A capitulative JE for being aware of its nullity.

I hesitate before the narrative that is mine, has in part been imposed on me, and that I have committed too much time already to reinventing, despite the absurdity of this project that I wish were without markers but never ceases to be delineated by whichever authority, tearing words from my mouth, the only context I may call mine, and toward which I may turn for assurance.

Several lines more, from *L'Injure* this time, a text that undid me, that doesn't *correspond*, that solicits no answer – in order to shake myself from my silence, in order to speak of the breadth of this against-which : *Tu n'es rien. / Tu n'es ni le lieu d'où tu viens ni celui vers lequel tu te diriges. [. . .] Tu n'es Rien. Sans ta ville tu n'es Rien. Pourtant entre ses murs tu n'es que du gibier et même les omnivores, même les rapaces se passent de toi. Tu te grises de mépris et te rassasies de nausée.*

Tu n'es Rien.[17] A brutality, this text that swallows what it spits up, in a vain attempt to detach itself from *le désir, suffocant, inexécutable, de nommer.*[18]

What the residual reveals of nothingness as transmitted by the photograph – *la folie qui menace sans cesse d'exploser au visage de qui la regarde*[19] – has an *edificial* linguistic foundation : that is, if it isn't already, it is in the process of becoming a scrap, a vestige, a *ruin* : the sum of what we are. Architecture of lack, of loss that is the desire cum delirium of disappearance : the passage from nothingness to nothingness.

Is it possible not to question this nothingness? Not to be appalled by it, resist it? Not to cry out : *What do you mean, no?*

---

[17]*You are Nothing. / You are not the place from which you come nor the place toward which you go. [. . .] You are Nothing. Without your city you are Nothing. Yet between its walls you are only bait and even the omnivores, even the vultures pass over you. You are drunk with disdain and gorge yourself full of nausea. You are Nothing.*

[18]*. . . the suffocating, inexecutable, desire to name.*

[19]Roland Barthes, *La chambre claire. Note sur la photographie*, Paris, Éditions de l'Étoile, Gallimard, Le Seuil, 1980. (*. . . the madness which keeps threatening to explode in the face of whoever looks at it.* Trans. Richard Howard, *Camera Lucida*, New York, Hill and Wang, 1981.)

The residual compromises the achievement of wholeness and disappearance in their absolute entirety. It recalls our state of suspension in space and time; it reduces while elevating, it deduces, from what it destroys, what we are, have been; as though only the disappearance of the trace were in a position to convince us of its tracing. We pursue, quietly, exhausted : *There, I was*. With little conviction, incapable nonetheless of disentangling from the borrowed trajectory.

In the features of Claude Cahun's face, I encounter the echo of what's left of me. In reality, it is quite the vexing opposite, what of myself is returned to me, is, in her, residual, belongs to her, might (as well) belong to her. At least, in the (arbitrarily) closed space of exchanged looks, of crossed bodies, the transposition of features muddles what of each of us would otherwise be distinct, the support we find ourselves looking for when each we say : *JE*. By claiming a separate space, we consign ourselves (inadvertently) to the envelope sealing us to the dispatch that awaits, that we convey. Expedition of the absence that misleads me, mourning unmoored, *peau de chagrin* tightening to the point of suffocation. But here is the paradox of the liaison whose aim might be a shared *distinction*, a desired complicity, a wrenching voluptuousness : correspondence returns me invariably to myself, isolates me from the thing, the place, the effort made to remove myself over this distance of distress inviting the body to its pain, the earth to the sea, the mouth to aridity. *Nowhere* is none other than me, folded incessantly over the place – the stare – that obliges me to oblivion without, however, allowing me to forget everything I have been through (and what has been through me), everything of the past, of History, what remains and what summons me, everything that subsists of the nauseated regurgitated thing, all the language stuffed inside and which formulates me against what I am, might be.

Nothingness is the place where we recognise ourselves. The residual, the movement that brings us back from there. Desire, the trial that holds us, the point of suspension : incapacity (stupor). The letter, distance, begun. The stare, the conductor so to speak – an interminable, multidirectional, proliferating circuit of burnt bridges, the very opposite of a city map . . . the *mis*direction devoid of cross streets leading insolently back to the seductive, unrecognisable point of departure, which isn't one because it happens that it is the echo of a place transported there where we have the gall, confusedly, to show up.

(1 5) What summons me

Earlier I said : the sum of what we are. Have I even the right to appropriate, to summon, to assume the presence of some collectivity, suggest even the slightest degree of *belonging* (even minute, between clearly indicated parentheses), to conjecture implicitly on the relationship between you and me, in order to broaden my terms, say we from the JE I have already declared to be unstable, hopeless, disconcerting, crushed under the weight of all sorts of disorders? To insinuate you *there* where (uncomfortably) I place myself, not only in addressing these words to you, drawing you into the error that intimates me, in the shattering wind of a desire without itinerary, of a world without cover, a battering invective, but to make you the guarantor of this JE, call you to witness, implicate you, at last, in my own affliction, afflict you with what mustn't necessarily take *place*?

I do think so, yes.

Yes, but (a small breach allowing for the termination of the contract, a nimble turn of phrase holding you to the word while at the same time saying *Let go* . . .)

It is a question of . . . touch. I was going to say : a *problem* of touch. I would be mistaken to approach it in this way, to try, with this phraseology, to maintain some distance, to intellectualise the thing I have under my skin, skimming all of my senses (this way and that, and often unconsensually) :

you, *toi*. To problematise what is not without consequence, but whose problematics arise, not from *touch* itself but from the relationship maintained with this *assemblage*, my reception of it, the invective, the collapse, in a single place, of all the treacherous constitutive places, beginning with that which is in no position to claim to belong to a veritable, ordinary, beginning, a *first place*, seconded : the body.

Encounter – even failed (can it be otherwise?) – is such that it institutes an economy of exchange, the same economy that models it. Touch is its currency : scrapes and excesses of rage, tribadism and gropes, grunts and penetration, the surfaces that constitute and summon us, introduce themselves surreptitiously, like illness, or exaggeratedly, like a fire; that impulse and enflame us, embarrass. Touch that incites intolerable wrenching, because what comes to me abandons me, taking with it a bit of flesh. The sublimated isolation encloses us in the *inhabited* place where we are : surrounded by people. If by chance we speak to mirrors, it is perhaps less for narcissistic reasons than out of a desire for *dead time* separating us from the battering voices we carry. I turn the page of a book and an entire civilisation harasses me. If I must accuse myself, I can only do so by drawing you with me into my mind's maze where I love of a love worthy of misanthropy.

So this touch, this sometimes conflictual contact that absorbs us *sensorially*, engaging desire, revolt or indifference, inflicts both the residual and nothingness, the residual that *includes* nothingness and that which emerges from it. The displacement, the reorientation, that result from these encounters, and are subsequent to encounter itself, to the correspondence begun by encounter, instigate the madness of disorientation. There is the certainty that the encounter took place, and an inability to situate it, to situate oneself in relation to it, to say *here* with conviction or resolve, to move toward an envisionable elsewhere. Mad nothingness hollowing into the body, whatever its position – generous or revolting – relative to touch. Touch is a substitute for, *becomes*, indeed *is*, the passage from nothingness to nothingness. The strangeness, what makes of me a stranger, adding itself to touch become nothingness, whose *habitual* character does not, however, diminish its own curiosity, is this : from deep in the abyss, in the place that is not place, where nothingness takes place, overthrowing my points of reference, pulling the ground out from under my feet, convincing me not only of the spatial nullity through which I move; from nothingness to nothingness comes the residual – the remains, the vestige of abandon that encounter (touch) demands of me, urging me far from the thing that I see, that I live, feel, madly.

From nothingness, *this*. Wrenches, wildly.

(1 6) Over here

Am I in danger of straying from my subject, of losing my
way through my very sinuous argumentation? I do hope so.
How could I articulate the unfeasibility of a trajectory with-
out myself becoming lost in it? How could I situate myself
within a problem without being bogged down, misled, flat-
tened by it? Without being able to see further than the im-
age, the photograph in front of my face, which takes up all
the space including that which I reserve : *for myself.* Far be it
from me to claim to an overall view, when the idea of cohe-
sion is itself suspect. How is it possible not to lose language
while articulating the absence encrusted in the language
to which we lend ourselves (that we borrow), and poorly
at that, but with attention, even in constant collision with
muteness in wait, and intimated. Muteness exacerbated by
a dilapidated voice that reaches sorely toward it, untranslat-
ably, intolerably.

(1 7) Estrangement

The we I argued over returns me with several detours to
The City. Without ever becoming accustomed to them, I am
struck by the uses made of it, in other words, the distances
maintained – the illusion of these distances – in relation
to it, to The City, the place *par excellence* through which
we move, are moved. The sense of estrangement encoun-
tered between its walls, between its gates[20] distinguishes
itself from Baudelairean flânerie or Situationist dérive, in
that estrangement is indissociable from the city in which it
takes place. Flânerie offers the (bourgeois) figure of a cer-
tain spectacular detachment, and while maintaining a rela-
tionship with the aleatory shares with the dérive a certain
programmatism.

The estranged body is estranged *in* The City, estrange-
ment being a function of The City. It is incapable of main-
taining a distinction before The City which it becomes, and
to which it is assimilated. Consequently, The City, itself

---

[20]. . . (even when they are fictional, because many cities no longer have func-
tional gates, having at one point or another done away with them, or if they
have maintained them, with rare exceptions – Jerusalem, for example, which
comes to mind, where in addition to being violently guarded, the gates also
ensure a racialised, nationalist organisational structure – they now often
serve as adornment, like the Portes de Paris, decorative vestiges ensuring
a certain touristic pleasure, and attesting to a drained historical trajectory,
the archeological evolution of the city) . . .

a *corpus*, acts on the body that traverses it. The inside is absorbed into the outside, one is but the exposition of the other; despite themselves, body and City end up speaking (to) one another, arguing, struggling: space (here) is at stake. One and other are meeting places and touch with malice, discontent and delight.

Estrangement *corresponds* with The City. It might be the means by which one would approach the other, for The City approaches the body as much as the reverse occurs. I would go so far as to say that one *is* the other, one is an integral (bodily) part of the other. Its limbs, its words, its gestures and exhalations exist *in relation* to the gutters, sewers, scaffoldings and masonry. The City is the body's scaffolding, just as the body furnishes the scaffolding for the book as it is written. A confused, tilted, twisted scaffolding, no doubt, but implicated nonetheless. This observation is not only of a symbolic order; The City, which is concomitantly akin to the monument and the scrap, is a presence, and to say presence is to say consequence. It is the consequence of a labour, the work of hands. It is the consequence of a convergence, in one place, of several bodies and historical moments, of violence and voluptuousness, of desire and ravages, distrust and regret. To say City is to say feat and defeat, to say encounter, to say body and rise, metal and fall. The bodies, agglomerated into a City, leave their imprints, which return to us (and us to them) as we move through it. The raised wall,

the suspended bridge, the poured tarmac, come, with as-
sured displacement, from ourselves. Estrangement, manifest
as much corporeally – the corporeality of The City, of the
body that moves along its avenues – as it is psychologically
–affective estrangement, a sort of dissociation, disjuncture
of the senses – might be the result of this dislocation, the
oblivion that surfaces (in) us and through which we recall
what, of the city, now disappeared, enters by these (di)ver-
sions. (Di)versions effected and undertaken by clearing, by
deciphering, always ephemerally, the momentous moment
that fixes and wrenches with its grinding work, and where
the present takes place with persistent displacement.

(1 8) There

I will speak to you of a city, but which one? I was going to say : *my* city, but the possessive disturbs me. It lies. It lies twice : by association and in number. As much as there isn't only one city, I cannot say mine – of any of them. I hesitate, am reluctant.

Of Barcelona, what hold me are the unfortunate birds of Las Ramblas, the sky at dusk over La pedrera. Of Donostia, the white of its bridges, Urumea. Of Ljubljana, the reflections of the Ljublanica, the melting snow, a beat. Of Paris, the funiculaire, a sharp disappointment. Of New York, a crushing noise. Of Norwich, the River Yare, too many absences. Of Orio, an anchor, drizzle. Of Saint Jean-de-Luz, red tile, a bathtub overflowing with dishes, a disappearance. Of Zarautz, a voice, not mine, the littoral. Of Chicago, birds, buried, a death, always a death. Of Iowa City, nothing but white. Of Montréal, a plate in pieces, the mountain, fleeting. Of Toronto, a hunger. Of Lyon, a massacre, an extremity. Of the silenced city, a garden, a quarry.

It could be altogether otherwise.

Speak to you of a city but what for? To speak of its passages, its proximity, to speak of its scaled hills and constructions, to speak of its permeability, to bear witness to the dismantled, desirous body, to speak of its abandon and its rigidity. To speak of the unexpected, the fulfilled, unavowed encounter, postponed. To speak of what escapes, emotion, a hold, squalls and squalor. What remains of me, what departs, gains (on) me.

Speak to you of a city to underscore the aleatory and imprisonment; breath, a wager, engagement. And the awkward question of correspondence, its dependence on the grid. Does the city make possible the connection, maintained over distance through the epistolary without which, I do believe, (and I cite this example because it comes violently to mind), Marie Dorval, her lover, would never have erupted into George Sand's room at midnight declaring (herself) : C'est moi![21]

Speak to you of a city to speak to you of the trial of tracing, of touch, the force of the echo, place folded back, out of the body, the letter that allows me to situate (myself), the synergy of several movements at once toward a dispersed centre, and what I retain of it – despite myself, despite my estrangement – in other words, encounter : there.

I insist on the silenced city, on the part that escapes, on oblivion, regret, disappearance, for with Claude Cahun, I believe, as much as these painful consequences are inescapable, they are also cruelly *necessary*. From the other century,

[21]Joseph Amber Barry, *Infamous Woman: The Life of George Sand*, Garden City (NY), Doubleday, 1977. (*It is I!*)

December 1933 : "J'admettrais donc avoir vécu au travers sans la voir, cette rencontre *capitale*, si de la nommer ainsi ne m'indiquait assez qu'on ne peut y survivre."[22] Leading me to ask: do we indeed survive The City? (which is to say *encounter*, because The City is encounter, it makes encounter possible, it *demands* it); and furthermore, is it even possible, now, in light of all of our trajectories, in the present of our suppressed absences, to live *without* it, to extract ourselves from its repetitions, impasses and deviations, to exile it from the body where it is so (un)comfortably settled?

---

[22]Claude Cahun, "Quelle a été la rencontre capitale de votre vie?", dans *Minotaure*, n° ¾, December 1933; in *Écrits*, ed. F. Leperlier, Paris, Jean-Michel Place, 2002. (I would therefore admit to having lived through this *capital* encounter without noticing it, if to name it in this way were not indication enough that it cannot be survived.)

(1 9) Coarse corporeality

The photograph that falls so heavily upon me doesn't re-
motely allow for answers to these questions – besides, an-
swers are of no interest, they mislead thought, in addition
to which they encourage misguided assurance, contempt-
ible lethargy. If I distrust answers, I – carelessly? – invite
blunder, the awkwardness without which it would not be
possible to go further, the vexing uncertainty that upsets the
idées reçues in which, in the face of all opposition, we bathe
involuntarily. Still, it (the photograph) allows me to enlarge
the site of questioning, while narrowing my focus, entirely
captivated as it is (as I am) by the intensity of the stare that
fixes mine. The book, having left the shelf, is now installed,
somewhat permanently, on my work table where it swallows
the bit of room that's left.

Much emptying was required to arrive at this book of
absence, at this space from which and in which it is written
– in which I write it. Space hollowing me in favour of the
thing that risks swallowing me whole, *replacing* me. And is
this not the insidious role played by our antecedents, our
anteriority, even those unknown to us? Attraction, desire,
come precisely from that which is destructive, ravaging. The
promise – because desire often takes the form of a promise,
however poorly kept – is, to begin with, a promise of fixa-
tion (a relational, temporal, geographical, sexual fixation, as

well as photographic). It guarantees a *place*. It situates us in relation to those having preceded us in time (and in death). Logically, this place should, therefore, assure us of an *existence*, for what are our antecedents if not our genitors, male or female, the generative effort that makes of us the sum of what we are, or as I have previously corrected myself : what summons us. My experience of the thing is quite the vexing opposite.[23] What I feel, far from some sense of assurance, is more reductive than generative : the disappearance, the erasure of everything toward which this movement should project me. Fixation, yes, but in the sense of imprisonment. Fixation, in other words, strain : the place that is reserved for me, in the lineage that is not offered but imposed, (that purports to offer itself in imposition), is already taken by what will be made of me, and not by what I am, or *might be*, nor by what I do, might do. Coarse body of experience, grafted onto this surface I haven't chosen. In addition, besides imposing their own (im)proper framework in a (fictitious) future of their own design, these antecedents, this anteriority, operate an assured regression, obliging at least to a double trajectory; on the one hand in order to undo

---

[23]I am drawing from my experience now rather than on some generality that isn't mine to claim; besides, there is ample evidence already of what the *cogito* did to Descartes, and to us all, heirs caught in the furrow of his unthinkable – *irreparable?* – thought, of his decreed generality.

ourselves from the first, inflicted; on the other, to find our own, the many possible trajectories, which will estrange themselves and which we will choose or not choose to find again or to let go. All of which, of course, rests on a highly supervised linguistic chain, carefully formulated, where what is fixed in time coagulates in the mouth. The photograph of Claude Cahun is, of course, not solely responsible for this degradation. The shock comes from its function as *reminder*, oddly making her into an ally, my companion on this path of extraction, of refusal, of emancipation, all of which . . . desired. What (s)he accuses (s)he proclaims. So much voluptuousness in this volatile field!

The power relations maintained with these antecedents require a semi-continual reiteration of the JE we come to claim for ourselves. Because the JE is otherwise always preceded by these other *je*, assembled into a vapid collectivity-cum-faction, removing in this way any possibility of JE, any possibility of trajectory, of directionality, of choice. Such that the face that might be mine melts into that of the genitor or older sibling, their *im*proper violences, whose continuity is ensured by my countenance. Echoing Bataille, I have already said so : *to resemble oneself is to disappear*. The antecedents that trail after us promise it, guarantee it, ensure it, injury.

It is clear, I think, having come this far in the muddle I am making for myself and which imbricates me with it, that what, of the divided trajectory of this text hold me – what swallow me especially – are the hollows, the drains, the gaping openings resulting from touch, from encounter, from correspondence, the cæsuræ that interrupt its functioning, rather than what might (ful)fill or satisfy them.

When, in *La Pesanteur et la Grâce*, Simone Weil evokes the void necessary for the presence of grace, she writes : "La grâce comble, mais elle ne peut entrer que là où il y a un vide pour la recevoir, et c'est elle qui fait ce vide."[24] Against the *promise* (and the premise) of fulfillment, are the often determining collisions, the struggles led against, expressions of *resistance*.

The void's malleability, its fluidity, are consistent with water's suppleness, its vigorous, even obliterative capacity. It enrapts and submerges, batters and engulfs. Its surface, a surface of longing and discord – disagreement – is saturated with the absence of the thing, once present, anticipated, whose trace, stolen away, subsists; not visible, nor altogether

---

[24]Simone Weil, *op. cit.* (*Grace fills empty spaces but it can only enter where there is a void to receive it, and it is grace itself which makes this void.* Trans. Emma Crawford.)

disappeared: the thing, precisely, that provokes a kind of madness that language is certainly incapable of accounting for.

Our stammers float at its surface; the reflection returned to us is that of our own face accosted by the void, not Weil's capricious void, but the undecided, bruised and unaccomplished void, from which we emerge, from which we are not done emerging, and which urges us for the duration of our lives.

The nothingness evoked earlier (the place where we recognise ourselves) continues to work us over, to accomplish its underhanded task through the residual (the movement that brings us back). A most certain aporia[25], where the outlet is but provocation and simply roots us (me) further in quicksand, a ravaging seabed whose tide spits us up onto a fractured shore, ceaselessly breaking apart the trajectory with which we might identify, the body that might be ours, the detail of an eye resting by chance there, where there is not, there, where nothingness has not finished catching up with us.

---

[25]Sarah Kofman, *Comment s'en sortir?* Paris, Galilée, 1983. "Traduire, s'ouvrir un chemin dans une langue en utilisant ses ressources, décider pour *un* sens, c'est sortir des impasses angoissantes, aporétiques de toute traduction. C'est accomplir le geste philosophique par excellent, un geste de trahison. Reconnaître l'intraductibilité de *poros* et d'*aporia*, c'est indiquer qu'il y a dans ces termes [...] de quoi rompre avec une conception philosophique de la traduc-

Hollows, drains, cæsuræ : are these liminal spaces, psycho-linguistic littorals that tear away language, dig more deeply into the horror of our own disappearance – anticipated, lived, remembered? Three tenses collapsed into one, and whose formulation, this tongue, our tongues, deny; whose elocution our tongues break?—

Disappear for speak, hollow for bind, littoral for fall. Territories repulsed by our devastated constructions.

---

tion et avec la logique de l'identité qu'elle implique). [...] Dire que *poros* est un chemin à frayer sur une étendue liquide, c'est souligner qu'il n'est jamais à l'avance tracé, toujours effaçable, toujours à retracer de façon inédite." (17-18). (Translation, opening a way in a language by making use of its resources, deciding on *one* sense, is to exclude the anguishing, aporetic impasses of any translation. It is the accomplishment of the philosophical gesture *par excellence*, a gesture of treason. Recognising the untranslatability of *poros* and *aporia* is to indicate that there is in these terms [...] cause to break with a philosophical conception of translation and with the identitarian logic that it implies. [...] To say that *poros* is a path to be frayed across a liquid expanse is to underscore that it is never traced in advance, always erasable, always to be newly retraced.)

(2 1) One name conceals another

Je est un autre wrote that other cited to the point of saturation. As though to dispense himself of that responsibility. To make direct contact with chaos without ever having to designate anything in his *proper* name. A name it is damningly impossible to forget, in the sometimes narrow field of letters, saturated as it is with literaries. To say *other* in order to remove himself from the intolerable display case of his *je*, to exonerate himself of his words, silence the objections of his superego, declaim against his attachments, lash out *freely*.

The name Cahun conceals at least one other name : the name of the father – Schwob. Suzanne Malherbe, Claude Cahun's lover, offers herself Marcel Moore as an additional self. Illustrator of some of the writings of Cahun who takes her own pictures (falls for her JE) from which (s)he meets me over all these years of distance, summons me without warning from the book that I call to me, suits me, suffers me, squeezes me in her there. Nathanaël, then, that I choose for myself, am, one for other, away from Stephens, the patronym, behind which lurks a complicating Cohen. Whereas I might risk the permanent loss of my voice, my without-which, my cities overlaid into a single here-there, the admonishment that awaits me. Even, we are even, but History has not finished taking us in (to its arms).

So many translations summon just as many deaths. Am I not kneading the ashes of my speech, anticipating their decay, when conveying the vestiges that confront me? grinding my own bones? and what right have I to drag someone else's name there, if only her photograph, and what does (s)he want with me anyway? Nathanaël does not exist either, it is well documented, our uprisings attest to this, *here* and *there*, we are standing, with our pants down, the door slammed in our faces, a cold wind at our backs. Still, the trap that would assimilate us to the real is the means by which we would escape from it, the gap that presents the interrupted, postponed, manipulated, incorporated choice of succession, of geographies, of temporality, of formulations, of appetites – all of which are . . . predisposed. In the end, is it a matter of asking : Where am I and how? Or rather . . . But what is my there?

(2 2) There for therefore

I will speak to you of a madness. It is inscribed in the lines of a face copied out a hundred times on transparent paper thrown to the fire. The fire is me, is you, is whosoever opens, looks, approaches, becomes inflamed. An impostor at the edge of the book, seized by the anguish of continuance, a desire verging on insanity, the effect, not of a torrent, but of the effort that holds it back, contains it; the beat, the stammer, in the face of what cannot, will not, express itself, framed and serving as a frame. There is closure, enclosure and dismemberment. There is duration, grafted onto temporality rent by our experience of it. The shiver is of the present. The present of corporeality. The body of madness. Madness maladdressed. I fall upon the demolition site of thought. I follow the decomposed pipes. I take note of the rust, the grease, the tar, the piss, the coal, the pylons, the birds' nests, the hinges, the frames, the tiles, the embellishments, the dead, the pieces. The river, the hill, the pier, the shore, the sea, the village, the quarter, the surroundings. No need to mark it all down. To draw the debris all the way to me. To order it, repatriate it, (re)sell it. Impossible to be rid of it. To make nothing of it, to sublimate it into me.

Nothingness is all that. There. Baited, I say : *there*. Abated.

fondement langagier édificiel :
s'il ne l'est ~~pas~~ déjà, il est en
voie de devenir un reste, un
vestige, une _ruine_ (ce que
nous sommes).

FoLie

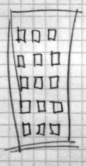

le passage du rien au rien

THE BOOK I AM COMING TO

( )

Madness for flight. It turns (in) me.

I employ several strategies at once. I embellish. I conceal. I arrange. I disturb. I solicit. I repel. (Repeal). The state of things is such that I unfold the envelope and gently remove its contents, themselves wrapped in protective paper. Despite the care taken on either end, what I hold in my hands is already sadly distorted by the distance it has had to travel. I transport it as far as the garden, whose lush chaos could only have come from the body, the body that is not earth, but a thing transported here with me. I bury it.

In the end, it is quite possible that I am mistakenly asking (myself) the question of *belonging*, of *situation*, of the profound and dislocating disjuncture that opposes body to place, body to any space which would assimilate it : City, estrangement, encounter. Or else that the question asks me in a context to which I have no right of access. I say that *It turns (in) me.* Is this then the articulation of the abyss against which I must defend? The sum and foundation of the terror that haunts? Madness indeed if the revulsion (revolution?) that accompanies the turn divulges, declares so complacently the nature of the lure. Is it at any moment possible, or even desirable, to turn back? Might the terror experienced before this or that situation (this photograph, to return to it) come precisely from my inability to hold back the energy that propels me, has already propelled me, that once launched, it is impossible to extract myself from the gesture – whether unexpected or determined – that presses us into the wounding trajectory. Wounding, in part, because it announces the disintegration of that which it draws to itself without destroying its trace, without affirming it either. The question that needs asking, that injures me at the same time as the trajectory provoked by the particular photograph from which I cannot undo nor defend myself, alongside the question asked earlier – *What is my there?* – might possibly be : Is it ever possible to return from there? More immediately, to turn away from what turns (me) away? To turn back? Faced with the inevitable uninhabitable, I must at very least spit up, rail against, the thing that leaves such a bad taste, that I abhor, but that abhors me even more. And by whose right? The one I grant myself.[26]

---

[26]The recent turn-of-the-century spilled into this one (whose aleatory determination doesn't impress me one bit – why measure the passage of time in this way; or rather why pass time like this? if not, of course, in order to recall the knell of all those religions at once as a distraction from their horrible deformity), a century speciously saturated with academicism, is overpopulated with vapidness to such a degree that it is impossible, and certainly not recommended, to think for oneself (and what might that mean?). Where, without the endorsement of the Greats of even the recent past, we keep our mouths and asses shut before the thing that wishes to express itself, but which, just like you, is bullied by its own fear of the menacing shadow of a madness of global proportions that sleeps in your insomniac slumber.

It turns (in) me. Do we (re)turn from there, the place that turns (in) us? Do we (re)turn from ourselves, our own divergences, our multiplicity – dividedness –, the encounters that ensure both interruption and continuity? Do we (re)turn from the place that turns (in) us and cannot be specified? Does the JE know how to retrace those steps in the furrow of the echo that transforms everything in its wake, even its substance, the quality that makes the echo what it is? Do you know?

What is it about return? Who traces its trajectory? And the other's? And the lure's? What, of each of us, *remains* in the space opened at the moment of approach, before arrival, in the between always desirous of arriving, wanting desperately for the arrival which will empty of sense, of sensuality, what will have been emptied, *there*, to the end, but never ending?

Madness might indeed stem from my incapacity, my *refusal*, at the heart of a system that exacts such demands, to situate myself in relation to the dictated primacy of an inculcated *origin*, whose generative impulse, in appearances generous, serves *before all* to claim – at a very high price – the part of me it will have artificially granted. Madness, which, in sum, is not madness at all but designed in this way by a network of systems fashioned against every possibility of *spillage*, voluptuousness, touch. That works *against* the body that constitutes it; in other words that doesn't recognise what it is made of, makes of itself, undoes.

The suffering – preceded by a mess of emotions, where it is necessary to leave room for a sort of exhilaration accompanied by sharp distress – the suffering that suffuses as I approach the photograph of Claude Cahun is provoked in part by the recognition, even the admission, that what (s)he offers me of myself, what (s)he restitutes in a sense, is immediately stolen back, but not without first having been stolen from herself; that the restitutional gesture carries the articulation, the recognition of that which, incomplete, provoked the restorative gesture. The lure of the latter is that recognition resides in the denial of the mended thing, of the blinding vestige from which we attempt to protect ourselves, even, and I would say especially, when it looks us in the face, where, *there*, we prefer to ignore it, we cover our eyes, we look *elsewhere* than there, where we are, would be, and blindly. It recalls that which, there before us, has disappeared, is no more, without our being able to offer it (ourselves) to restorative oblivion. The tear, disjuncture, strangeness, estrangement, dissolution . . . might suggest that absence, I submit to the (in)tangible evidence, might be the scrap of myself before the incomprehensible disappearance of what goes away, that I (JE) claim (for myself) stubbornly, vociferously, at the top of my voice, and to the point of extinction.

( )

Enough of this train of thought. It has worked me over to excess. At present the photograph is nothing more than a wall against which to lean with force, an unshakable surface that, as object, only entrenches the relationship I maintain with it. I have become overly accustomed to it. It invites a dissociative relapse and I no longer see the thing I am looking at; I no longer see the quality of the stare that meets mine. It is no longer clear that this is an encounter, nor that it takes place in a direct and mediated way, drawing with it a whole history that, I admit, I am incapable of accounting for. Book open or closed, eyes alienated and haunted, by offering myself to it day after day before this screen, I am becoming disillusioned by it, I am *ceasing* . . . to pay attention.

I have so often declared that it is not possible to pass without injury from one language to another. I was meaning translation, translation in the first degree, so to speak, the one that operates the redistribution of a text into a language other than the one in which it was composed; leaving aside artistic, cultural, industrial – metaphorical – translations (not with the purpose of marginalising or deligitimating them) between media, from body to word, from image to speech, from machine to canvas, from galley to book, from blueprint to building, from hand to rock, alchemy of senses and matter. In short, translation in its most restricted, habitual sense, which does not preclude the site of this work from being rabidly contested. And why not? It is a territorial matter, and to say territory is to say limits and ferocity, hierarchy and coloniality, pettiness *oblige*. No passage without injury because of the manifold breakages sustained by body and word and the danger, ever present, of a catastrophic blockage at the moment of emergence on the other side; rupture, hemorrhage. No passage without injury because of the multidirectionality of the explosive, divided reach, which opens, closes, and fuses together several movements at once, which collide, from within imposed limits, with the unlimitable unstable, burst, sutured and torn. A text, offered in this way to its decomposition and to its recasting in a space removed from the one in which it makes – made – itself, inevitably risks a dislocation whose effect is exposure to an irrefutable disorientation that, through breakage and destruction, invites an additional (re)constitution.[27] Texts speak to one another all at once, and that incalculable din

---

[27]*Cf.* "WANT: L'INTRADUISIBLE", in *At Alberta*, Toronto, BookThug, 2008. "Our translational struggle (at the edge of what river? by whose hand bruised? and in what name?) locates itself, failingly, within untranslatability – within the untouchable, unspeakable reserve of desire coiled in the belly of our texts, in the place where, imperfectly, they come to touch one another; the lines that we cross, the gulf that swallows us. And it is here, in this gulf, this abyss, here, which I called to begin with 'the failure of translation', from here this failure that desire emerges, only here that desire can emerge, if at all." (33-34)

of tangled voices is a seabed, a planetary silence, a puddle of water, from which I emerge scratching my head, saying (to myself) : *Je veux l'intraduisible* . . . not in order to silence them but to seize them otherwise, so that the distance, so many times undertaken, with, on my tongue, the echo that delivers me, incarcerates, embeds me, will make of absence, of the incomprehensible, a terrible, tranquil, devastating tenderness. *I want what no language holds.*

I want : *there is not.* The thing, the there; expressive, attenuated, bursting. I place myself there, my body positioned awkwardly, smugly, between two books, between manifold texts, between languages projecting from bodies in which they don't hold anymore. Incapable of holding them back, we repulse them, reject them, diminish them; they surface out of *there* the body in which they remain nonetheless enclosed, unreachable, impassive, emotion-filled and mute, moving and concealed, dividing their course into proliferating trajectories, each of which unlocatable, grossly calculated, hazardous, immovable. At night, I dream only of them, their fusion, their impermeability, their flux. Circular circuits, impassable impasses, I render The City breathless as I move through it, to the end of the line, the top of the hill, the tumble down, where the whole thing starts from zero, augmented by the imprint that saturates me with the lure of its feasibility, the distance at every moment undertaken and postponed. Missed trains, rerouted buses, I notice too late, and the quarter hour becomes a fortnight, the familiar village unrecognisable, the neighbourhood turns to a rampart, I dive from the tops of buildings stretched toward a solid, shattering ground that opens at the last moment to engulf me, submerge me, liquefy, assimilate me, closing over as if nothing had happened. Two books if not two moments, two dislocated imprints, two bodies seized, accused, sanctioned, condemned, forgotten. Two for more because between them so many others in wait. Somewhere, over there, close by, elusive.

Two parentheses I said some time ago while nearby a life (an insufficiency of life) became smothered, an ordinary season unsettled the disposition of the senses. And the face that stared, stares at me, literally, steals this part of me.

Turns (in) me, returns (to) me, turns me out.

( )

Book unbegun (promising) or unopened, closed or mourn-
ed, perused or devoured, the book remains a voracity for
death overturned. Overturned, that is, displaced, but also
usurped, underhanded. The lure of the book is the lure of
every moment, (un)bound and misread. Each escapes us.
And we, of course, escape it as well : the *relationship*, the
liaison, the *correspondence* maintained with them (with the
present and its dislocations) simultaneously reiterate, su-
ture and detach, seize and collapse, echo and smother. All
this time, all these questions, would have been necessary in
order to arrive *there*, whose underside teaches us *there is not*,
distinguishable from *never*, in that its fractured construc-
tion is perpetually susceptible to drainage. The inevitable
uninhabitable attached to memory sewn into the skin of
the thing that escapes. The desire for (be)longing overcome
by an even stronger desire – to defend against it – rejects
the voluptuousness which would open all passages at once.
Leaving a space precisely for disjunctures and spillage. Out-
cry with neither trope nor even regret, or else saturated with
sadness, merging itself, body and discord, with the waters
that will submerge it, the littoral that will reshape it day after
day, consecrating it in the absorption and volatility of a mu-
table shore imprinted with every possible *there*. Conceived
and inconceivable. The never ending end of a gesture begun
without beginning, scattered, diffuse and gathered into the

uninhabited present of the inexhaustible desire of *there is* embraced by the JE that detaches from it : *desperately*.

As long as, in the very midst of a trajectory, we are on a verge of beginning, as long as we are in the space *between*, as long as we have not yet arrived, as long as we have not exhausted the vast expanse of movement, as long as, one way or another, the *there is not* is sought, as long as the place where we disappear ensures our continual disappearance, reassures us of it, as long as, spurred by the injurious desire that *turns (in) me*, we can say with the assurance that comes with having none at all : *there*.

The gesture of the book is the suicidal-murderous gesture that turns me back. Return is simply another crossing. The voracity for death overturned is the painful recognition of the inevitable uninhabitable upheld by a word that escapes, scarring, an unpronounceable word we have yet to encounter at the edge of a voice that doesn't know, doesn't recognise itself, other than in the unrecognisable echo, transformed. The book is possibly the *place*, the *there is not*, the *there*, at once exemplary, singular, banal. It is effluent and tributary. The first without arrival; the second without departure, repealing and amplifying one another, directed, but without real direction : aleatory.

The JE become other, intimated by the other burdened by the unstable exchange of names and identities, of *recognitions*, doesn't know whom to hold (accountable) anymore, doesn't know, in other words whom or what to speak to, *where* to begin, how to constitute *correspondence*. Reach remains caught in the hand from which it would extend, freely.

JE is (am) caught, taken, tried. Overturned. Turned in.

( )

There : not beyond, not before, but *affected*. Affected in every possible sense of the term without termination. Affected, that is, *overcome, afflicted* and *mad*. *There* : the place of our most debilitating disturbances, of our high aspirations, of our pains and our sufferings, excesses and mendacity, retreat.

I will speak to you of a book undelivered. Delivery without release. Without encumbrances. Deliverance for release, *It turns (in) me.* I don't emerge from *there* the place of which I speak, where I invite you, which invents me, invents you, boasts of itself, which arrives *there*, to you where I send it, will *enclose* me. When, from Brecht, the echo of his *An die Nachgeborenen*[28] arrives all the way *here*, it is already getting late, there is only *there is not* on which to lean the ruined head, the mad eyes, the rest of its voice, sensorial, scattered on a ground that wants to melt into the next fallen body : it will fall. I tally it all up, *in extremis*, at the end of a book, whichever one, where hands assemble to formulate the useless gesture of its continuation, carrier of vestiges that gorge the waterways, caverns and gutters of our prime detritus, of our infectious Cities. While guarding against naming what

---

[28]To those who come after.

or whom ever. I know them for having frequented them, and as a result none at all : slashed, rejected, defenestrated; plummeted from railings, bridges and balconies; swallowers of barbiturates, sleeping insomniacs, cancerous, stammered. Books undelivered, see. Survival, after which. That I read out loud quietly, mutterings of the end of time, the reminder, stinging, of the extremes toward which we mislead ourselves. What is that distance?

If I have one word to say, a single declaration to make, a single name to pronounce, it is the one, always, that doesn't come to mind, or too late, the receiver put back, the voice at the other end dissolved in the foreground noise that invites neither remembrance nor oblivion, but inattention, the fit of emotion that makes us answerable without requiring *a* presence : *there.*

( )

It has not been, is not, a matter of *revealing* nor *recounting* anything at all – obviously (obviately). If our literatures are saturated with confessionalism, anecdotalism, if psycho-charlatans rush at art in search of a fundamental truth, *in the name of a father* or a *castration*, and without consideration – this is *de rigueur*, in the name of an invented science[29] – for the sacked life, it is because we learn nothing of ourselves, preoccupied, as we are, with devotions to a course toward some purity, a *singularity* that would furnish the answer to a question of no interest, as if in total isolation (control), it were possible to breathe, think, move away from *every other thing*, resting with self-satisfaction on a piece of mind, the pillars of reasoning, the four walls of a rightly erected house. I ask your forgiveness. I ask you nothing.

Correspondence draws a line. Across us. We touch at a distance. To the point of irritation. Voluptuously bathed in our texts, retreating and estranged in our shivering, dismantled, reconstructed Cities.

Excuse me : this is no monument. But sharp, breaking. What comes to me withdraws. What enters by the mouth inhales itself, provokes the delirium against which I brace

---

[29](All science is invention.)

myself, disappear. If I had to choose, attach to this interruption – *the book I am coming to* – a word that could bear witness to the passage of what has passed, of the incomplete, erased, slaughtered, resurfaced past delivered *there* before me where I receive it with a certain dislocation with uncertainty and emotion, this, despite myself, despite the *there is not* of the inevitable uninhabitable, fully, madly, and without which : Touches. Touched me.

( )

Another thing. With your permission. I have already spoken at length of *appearance* and of *belonging*. Of the lure and the drain. The letter, unpublished, goes back far. It is illegible. With the innumerable revealed faces arrives a last one (not in the sense of a final one, but the most recent that I recall, that I happen to be evoking). At the risk then of contradicting myself . . . I will speak to you of a disappearance, an interruption which hasn't the form of a book, which is tendered and denied in the delirium of exchange within a *family story*, the fa ille in which meaning is degraded, ruins itself, where I silence the tremor of a secret in favour . . . but of what? What do they tell us, those who escape us? At one point I said History. In capital letters, I said it felt it, I hesitate before it : I don't know what to make of it, but it works me over, swarms me. The unspeakable history, I said, wrote, called out, of disappearance. *The details are of no importance. The book thickens otherwise. . . .*

I missed the occasion of an encounter. This one and many others as well. I no longer await it. It is of the order of the unknown, unknowable. I admit : some days, I would cross no bridge, I would not go to the water. Yet I dream it : the Seine, the Orio, the River Dart, the Saint-Laurent, so many rivers, but also : the Mediterranean.

(*There* : Oran, 1946. There are two days : the day of birth and the day of death. There is no beginning again. I know nothing beyond these two dates : 1938, 1946. Twice the unexpected. What remains : a city, a collaborator, two hands that tighten. The throat, theft, a death. Deft.)

I don't know where to turn. There are of course the many volumes of history – History – the accusations, testimonies, complicities. I have read some. Suffered some. Remember little. I have hesitated, raged, wept. I have done a lot of : nothing. I have written. Shoshana Felman reminds: *The inside has no voice.*[30] It is still necessary, I think, to guard against speaking for others. Claude Cahun doesn't need anyone – not me, not another – to have her word, besides which, (s)he has spoken (for her selves) exceptionally. So many intellectual movements have claimed her reductively in such a short time. One suggests, perplexingly, that Breton was the love of her life.[31] Another that the absent mother

---

[30]Shoshana Felman, "The Return of the Voice", in S. Felman and D. Laub, *Testimony: Crises of Witnessing in Literature, Psychoanalysis, and History*, New York/London, Routledge, 1992.

[31]Carolyn J. Dean, "Claude Cahun's Double", in *Yale French Studies*, No. 90, *Same Sex / Different Text? Gay and Lesbian Writing in French*, 1966. ("The entire book [*Claude Cahun: L'écart et la métamorphose*] is structured around a homology between this impossible relation and Cahun's putative, unrequited love for the surrealist André Breton, although Leperlier provides little if any evidence for that passion.")

was the obsessive impulse behind her artistic production. The lover, the mother's substitute. (In this very prudish bourgeois way, *incestuous homosexuality* is explained – named, pathologised[32]). Her photography comprised of self-portraits when it arguably constituted, at least in part, a collaborative project with Moore[33]. Cindy Sherman has been made, contestably, into the heir of this œuvre.[34] Cahun has become the precursor of the post-modern, of performativity. So much energy spent to contain her, rivet her to a closed space, restrained, besieged from all sides by the abject aspirations of my contemporaries.

(The child's name was Claude.)[35]

---

[32]Danielle Knafo, "Claude Cahun, The Third Sex", in *Studies in Gender and Sexuality*, Vol. 2, No. 1, 2001: ". . . as well as her incestuous homosexual desires (which found no outlet owing to her mother's absence)."

[33]*Don't Kiss Me: The Art of Claude Cahun & Marcel Moore*, ed. Louise Downie, New York, Aperture/Jersey Foundation Trust, 2006.

[34]Katy Kline, "In or Out of the Picture: Claude Cahun and Cindy Sherman", in *Mirror Images: Women, Surrealism, and Self-Representation*, ed. Whitney Chadwick, Cambridge, MA, MIT Press, 1998. "It is in their degree of participation in or removal from the world that Cahun and Sherman will be seen to diverge." Also: "Virginia Zabriskie remembers Cindy Sherman seeing Cahun's work on a visit to her New York gallery, but "long after she had begun making her own work. (In conversation, August 1996)."

Happily, there are exceptions to the *uses* made of Cahun, as of a product, neglected or overvalued, on a market artificially inflated by a desire for ownership, so often a synonym for understanding. (We are not so far from the adamic gesture of *nomination*, the very calculated scourge of this possessive, possessional West). Because, and the gesture has become so habitual that we are insufficiently taken aback by it, allowances are seldom made for the disjunctures between life and artistic contribution; one is exhibited as pathological evidence of the other, it is a reflex among right-thinkers today to nail autobiography to artistic expression, without recognition that the latter spills far beyond the former, that the body continues along its exhilarated, agonising way, and that, independently of it, works of art act like run-off, finding the form best suited to them as they fall where they may. If only, rather than appropriating them, we learned to speak to them, from the echo they offer of themselves, to find the passing form best suited to us. It is perhaps asking too much. I ask for more.

---

[35]"An affective detour: In the familial imaginary, Claude Cohen (1938-1946), son of Louisa (1908-2008), dead in Oran just after the birth of Francine (1945), occupies the space of unmarred potentiality, and of historical, communal martyrdom, a cypher for a kind of affective devastation; as with any telling or transmission, the language used to mark Claude's memory is a language of inevitable imprisonment, for the force of its potentiality lies precisely in the impossibility for him to consume, let alone consummate it. To speak, as it were, a name other than the one attributed to him." *At Alberta*, p. 63.

( )

Book. In the end I opened it. The book which from Lyon
crossed the ocean in a suitcase to end up continually on my
displaced, replaced book shelves; in four years, four cities,
seven dwellings, without counting the places of passage
(how am I to distinguish between dwelling and passage?)
The face that from the cover and spine of the book, a memo-
ry enfolded there without foundation, commands me, sum-
mons me, erases and injures me, anticipates me rigorously.
The promise, exhausted; desire, dizzying and damaged; the
book, the articulation of a botched suicide, postponed and
gravely pursued, of a crushed and restituted voluptuous-
ness, the voluble mouth pressed against the submerged
continent, the body split (spilt) over all of those borders,
claiming it for themselves, broken on the scaffold of mis-
understood, incomplete speech gathered into the fortuitous
gesture of encounter emerging from so many trajectories :
all traces combined. Unknown intruder, I introduce myself,
impostor, in the insidious trope of exclusion : I touch. I
erupt, interrupt, rupture. The book is a cæsura, uncondi-
tioned, it approaches and suffers being read, demands it.
If that which, so many times named, rejects and convokes
me, obliges me to my own disappearance, holds the muted
discourse of the aporetic impossibility of existence in and
of itself and in relation to an other, fleeting, in relation to
some *place*, desperately desired and successively fled, all the

coarse, imagined, uninhabitable places, it is also inevitably and inconsolably the divided trajectory made manifold through which I would situate myself in relation, *there*, to that which escapes, to Claude Cahun, who comes to me in the imperious anguish of a historical moment from which we have not finished emerging.

N. S.

Chicago 2006, 2008

(REMAINS)

MADDNESS

| . . . this sort of madness of interrupted movement . . . | I feel dread verging on madness. | And yet madness intrudes at the very moment at which the body can no longer tell itself from another, can no longer tell its constitutive dislocation, can't tell the differences required of it. | . . . the madness of disorientation. | Mad nothingness hollowing into the body . . . | . . . the thing, precisely, that provokes a kind of madness that language is certainly incapable of accounting for. | I will speak to you of a madness. | The body of madness. | Madness maladdressed. | Madness for flight. |

ECHO

| These words recall the echo emerging from a void . . . | A voiceless echo . . . | An echo, then, that resembles neither itself – because once projected it is transformed, deformed – nor the imitated sound, for being swallowed again immediately, ushered away from . . . me. | An echo, that is, a reply . . . | Voiceless echo, bodiless voice, unarticulated mouth. | . . . assimilated to the echo to which the echo returns . . . | . . . and whose removal is the very same echo that alludes to me. | . . . they return to the place of their refusal, of their expulsion, in the form of echoes entangled with all the places with which they might have . . . | The photograph is *echo*. | In the features of Claude Cahun's face, I encounter the echo

of what's left of me. | . . . because it happens that it is the echo of a place transported there where we have the gall, confusedly, to show up. | . . . the force of the echo . . . |

ABSENCE

| . . . whose vacancy, whose absence of content, attest to a linguistic void that can only express want, absence, retreat . . . | . . . and the absence, assimilated to the echo to which the echo returns, absence, in other words lacuna and want . . . | . . . who, by her absence, holds me, withholds me and that I hold in my hands . . . | . . . there is the total and totalitarian achievement of the absence to which I am confronted . . . | Absence of being and place . . . | The singular absence that is the text that denies us . . . | . . . inhabited by layers of absence of which we are one and none . . . | Expedition of the absence that misleads me . . . | . . . too many absences. | . . . in the present of our suppressed absences . . . | Much emptying was required to arrive at this book of absence . . . | . . . saturated with the absence of the thing . . . |

RUIN

| . . . a *ruin* : the sum of what we are. |

ENCOUNTER

| . . . this insatiate desire that announces every encounter
. . . | . . . the furtive and misunderstood place of *encounter* . . . |
. . . the JE evoked earlier, leads to *fortuitous* encounters . . .
| Hollowing the encounter is a drain . . . | . . . such that I
find myself asking whether this encounter did indeed take
place, if the possibility of this encounter might realisti-
cally be envisioned . . . | There is not only encounter, but
collapse. | Encounter – even failed (can it be otherwise?)
. . . | The displacement, the reorientation, that result from
these encounters, and are subsequent to encounter itself
. . . | There is the certainty that the encounter took place
. . . | . . . the remains, the vestige of abandon that encounter
(touch) demands of me . . . | To say City is to say feat and
defeat, to say encounter, to say body and rise, metal and fall.
| To speak of the unexpected, the fulfilled, unavowed en-
counter, postponed. | . . . in other words, encounter : there. |
". . . this *capital* encounter . . ." | . . . (which is to say *encounter*,
because The City is encounter, it makes encounter possible,
it *demands* it) . . . | . . . resulting from touch, from encounter
. . . | City, estrangement, encounter. | . . . the encounters that
ensure both interruption and continuity? |

CORRESPONDENCE

| . . . most certainly of a *correspondence.* | Of correspondence,

flight. | Correspondence for flight. | . . . this exchange, this relationship, this liaison, this *correspondence* . . . | . . . correspondence returns me invariably to myself, isolates me from the thing, the place, the effort made to remove myself over this distance . . . | . . . to the correspondence begun by . . . | And the awkward question of correspondence, its dependence on the grid. | . . . from correspondence, the cæsuræ that interrupt its functioning . . . |

CITY

| . . . an aggressivity that suffuses the skeleton of the cities through which we move . . . | . . . through several large U.S. cities . . . | Just like cities and the buildings that comprise them . . . | . . . the very opposite of a city map . . . | The we I argued over returns me with several detours to The City. | . . . because many cities no longer have functional gates . . . | . . . the archeological evolution of the city) . . . | . . . in that estrangement is indissociable from the city in which it takes place. | The estranged body is estranged *in* The City, estrangement being a function of The City . . . | . . . it is incapable of maintaining a distinction before The City which it becomes . . . | . . . The City, itself a *corpus* . . . | . . . body and City . . . | Estrangement *corresponds* with The City. | . . . for The City approaches the body as much as the reverse occurs. | The City is the body's scaffolding . . . | The City, which

is concomitantly akin to the monument and the scrap, is a presence . . . | To say City is to say feat and defeat . . . | The bodies, agglomerated into a City, leave their imprints, which return to us (and us to them) as we move through it. | . . . (of The City, of the body that moves along its avenues) . . . | . . . what, of the city, now disappeared, enters by these (di)versions. | I will speak to you of a city, but which one? | I was going to say : *my* city . . . | As much as there isn't only one city . . . | Of the silenced city, a garden, a quarry. | Speak to you of a city but what for? | Speak to you of a city to underscore the aleatory and imprisonment . . . | Does the city make possible the connection, maintained over distance through the epistolary without which . . . | Speak to you of a city to speak to you of the trial of tracing . . . | I insist on the silenced city . . . | . . . do we indeed survive The City? (which is to say *encounter*, because The City is encounter . . . | . . . my cities overlaid into a single here-there . . . |

WATER

| . . . and this chronology of travels dipped into all of those waters transformed itself into a moving mass that I dragged all the way to Chicago . . . | . . . consistent with water's suppleness, its vigorous, even obliterative capacity . . . |

BAIT

| Liaison for bait. |

DESIRE

| ... this insatiate desire that announces every encounter ...
| Desirous, it attempts to express its dislocation, intent on
joining what escapes it quite simply, but not without first
seizing (upon) it. | Mourning, melancholy, languor, desires,
perversions and languages find themselves juxtaposed with-
out any reason other than that which I grant them, capri-
ciously, intentionally. | ... Suppression of the desire that
spills from the body in which it is meant to remain enclosed,
unseated, silenced. | ... from the fragile breath of desire
... | ... *sense* (rejecting sensuality, and therefore the body,
desire) ... | ... away from the sole desire that may have
provoked it. | ... whence this desire, and why? | Where does
this desire come from? | ... to the look I desire ... | Archi-
tecture of lack, of loss that is the desire cum delirium of
disappearance : the passage from nothingness to nothing-
ness. | Desire, the trial that holds us, the point of suspension
... | ... in the shattering wind of a desire without itinerary
... | ... it is perhaps less for narcissistic reasons than out of
a desire for *dead time* ... | ... engaging desire, revolt or indif-
ference ... | ... of desire and ravages ... | Attraction, desire,
come precisely from that which is destructive, ravaging. | ...

because desire often takes the form of a promise, however poorly kept ... | ... a desire verging on insanity ... |

FA ILLE

Not so long ago, I pointed to the minute distance between la famille (family) and la fa ille (fault line ... flaw ... rift). | Between la famille and la fa ille, a letter comes to be absent, exposing the decline in question. | The fa ille might provide evidence of the defeat of the languages by which we might transmit ourselves ... | Fractured fa ille, the swollen tongue hooking on the remains of which it might otherwise settle, in breach of conduct, excised, split. |

M.

measure movement momentous moment mouth more mistakes make myself mind me move made muteness miroir most male materialised misunderstanding muddied might Montréal mountains Mediterranean moving mass moves mourning melancholy markers minute muddling months much museum mark mastodon milestones misuses much maintained manifest marrow Madness muddles minute mean misunderstood membership mythology monotheistic manifold meant maintain me matter materialisation mes moi mine meet mourned mislead

ESTRANGEMENT

| The sense of estrangement encountered between its walls, between its gates ... | ... in that estrangement is indissociable from the city in which it takes place. | The estranged body is estranged *in* the city, estrangement being a function of the city ... | Estrangement *corresponds* with The City. | Estrangement, manifest as much physically ... | ... (affective estrangement, a sort of dissociation, disjuncture of the senses) ... | ... despite my estrangement – in other words, encounter : there. | ... City, estrangement, encounter. | ... estrangement, dissolution ... might suggest that absence,

Cover: Detail from Le passage du rien au rien by Nathanaël
Interior and cover *typeslowly* designed

Still, for their attentions: Rachel Gontijo Araújo, Andrew
Blackwell, Amina Cain, Christopher Mattison

Image Credits:
Page 25 (top): Vitrine van den Bergh, launch of Aveux non
            Avenus (detail), June 1930; with the permission
            of Jersey Heritage Trust Collections.
Page 25 (bottom): N/N; Nathanaël, June 2006.
Page 66 : Le passage du rien au rien; Nathanaël, June 2006.

Library of Congress Cataloging-in-Publication Data

    Stephens, Nathalie, 1970-
    Absence where as : Claude Cahun and the unopened
    book / Nathalie Stephens (Nathanaël).
    p. cm.
    English and French (entre-genre)
    ISBN 978-0-9822645-0-8 (alk. paper)
    I. Title.
    PR9199.3.S7839A64 2009
    811'.54--dc22
    2008052501

Nightboat Books
New York
www.nightboat.org

NIGHTBOAT BOOKS

Nightboat Books, a nonprofit organization, seeks to develop audiences for writers whose work resists convention and transcends boundaries. We publish books rich with poignancy, intelligence, and risk. Please visit our website, www.nightboat.org, to learn more about us and how you can support our future publications.

Our books are available through Small Press Distribution. (www.spdbooks.org).

The following individuals have supported the publication of this book. We thank them for their generosity and commitment to the mission of Nightboat Books:

Jean M. Campbell
Katherine Dimma
Photios Giovanis
Elizabeth Madans
Rigoberto Gonzales
Prageeta Sharma
Benjamin Taylor

State of the Arts

NYSCA

In addition, this book has been made possible, in part, by a grant from the New York State Council on the Arts Literature Program.